The Art of FACT

Fast, Authentic Connections and Trust
A Modern Approach to Client Success through Genuine Engagement

Dr. Nicholas J. Pirro

The Art of FACT - Fast, Authentic Connections & Trust: A Modern Approach to Client Success through Genuine Engagement

Dr. Nicholas J. Pirro

The Art of FACT - Fast, Authentic Connections & Trust: A Modern Approach to Client Success through Genuine Engagement

Published by Pyrrhic Press Publishing

Highland Lakes, Vernon, NJ, USA

www.pyrrhicpress.org

Contact: editor@pyrrhicpress.org

Printed in the United States of America

Disclaimer:

This book is a work of nonfiction, created to share ideas and strategies for client engagement and relationship-building. While every effort has been made to ensure accuracy, the author and publisher assume no liability for errors or omissions, or any consequences related to the application of information contained in this book.

Acknowledgments

To my beautiful, incredible, and brilliant wife, my heartfelt thanks go to you. You are truly a Wonder Woman—my muse, and my guiding light. This book would not exist without your endless support, and insight. Your boundless patience and understanding have been my strength, and your love has been the heartbeat of my work. Thank you for standing by me, for believing in me, and for inspiring me in ways words can barely capture.

To my six extraordinary children, each of you is a part of this book and a source of my deepest pride. One of you is fiercely hard-headed and intelligent, pushing limits and expanding horizons. Another is discovering his voice and strength internally and externally, stepping into who he is meant to be. One of you is still searching for his place in this big, wild world, please do not repeat history, there are a million and one ways, find yours. While another is determinedly forging her own path and going at it to a drumbeat she regulates, in her own time and space. One has blazed an entirely new trail, done spectacular, seen the world and is soon to bring new life into the world. The greatest moms come from great moms; you have the best. And my youngest, thriving, is now fully at ease in her own skin, keep at it, you define your successful days. All my children, remember that your unique spirit, resilience, and individual journeys have been my inspiration.

This book is a tribute to all of you—my family. You have given me the foundation to create, the courage to pursue my dreams, and the joy that fills every page. Thank you for making life an incredible adventure.

Dedication

To my mother, whose legacy of teaching has extended beyond her years, leaving an indelible mark on my heart and mind. You instilled in me the values and virtues that shape who I am today, and it's because of your guidance, strength, and wisdom that I pursue every goal with determination and purpose.

Your belief in the importance of learning, your unshakable resilience, and your quiet yet powerful encouragement taught me to aim high, to persevere, and to strive for greatness. I owe you for so much of what I have become. This book, and every success a reader gains from it, is dedicated to you. Thank you, Mom, for lighting the path that I am so proud to walk.

Foreword

In a world where transactions often eclipse interactions, *The Art of Fast, Authentic Connections & Trust* is a timely guide. Dr. Nicholas J. Pirro has created more than a strategy here—he's crafted a philosophy. At a time when clients are not only aware of but actively seeking genuine connection, this book presents a refreshing, practical approach to meet this demand head-on. Responsive Resonance Theory, as Dr. Pirro calls it, isn't about shortcuts or quick fixes. Instead, it's about embracing a balance between swift action and genuine empathy to create a lasting impact in a fast-paced, competitive market.

Dr. Pirro introduces us to a method that bridges speed with sincerity. He invites us to step out of the transactional and into the relational. Drawing on his years of experience and nuanced understanding of human connection, he unveils a path for building trust at each step of the engagement process. His insights resonate with those who value depth in every conversation, who understand that the best partnerships aren't about selling but about aligning, listening, and delivering mutual value.

As you delve into this book, be prepared to shift your perspective on connection and engagement. This isn't just a book for sales professionals; it's for anyone looking to enhance their ability to relate meaningfully and authentically in any relationship, whether business or personal. Dr. Pirro's framework brings an intentional, empathetic focus to each step of the journey, empowering readers to create interactions that are not only effective but also genuinely impactful. Welcome to *The Art of Fast, Authentic Connections & Trust*—a guide to creating connections that last.

– Dr. Nicholas J. Pirro

Contents

Foreword 2

Chapter 1: What is Responsive Resonance? 3

Chapter 2: The Four Core Principles of Responsive Resonance 6

Chapter 3: The Step-by-Step Process of Responsive Resonance 9

Chapter 4: Quick Initiation – Building Momentum Fast 12

Chapter 5: Resonant Engagement – Deepening the Connection 13

Chapter 6: Maintaining Momentum and Curiosity 15

Chapter 7: Natural Closing Techniques 17

Chapter 8: Communication Best Practices 20

Chapter 9: Applying Responsive Resonance to Real-World Scenarios 23

Contents

Chapter 10: Evaluating Your Progress and Refining Your Style 27

Contents Cont.

Final Word 31

Reference Section for Responsive Resonance: The Art of Fast, Authentic Connection& Trust 32

About the Author 36

"The only limit to our realization of tomorrow will be our doubts of today." – *Franklin D. Roosevelt*

Chapter 1: What is Responsive Resonance?

Introduction

The world of sales is undergoing a major transformation. Gone are the days when a high-pressure pitch or scripted sales funnel was enough to win business. Today's clients are more informed, selective, and relationship-oriented than ever before. To stand out, sales professionals need to adapt, balancing the speed required in a fast-paced market with the genuine, person-centered approach that clients increasingly value. This evolution in the sales world has given rise to the concept of **Responsive Resonance**.

Responsive Resonance is a unique, adaptable approach to sales that combines the decisiveness of "Execute, then Think" with the depth of "Relational Resonance." In other words, it's about moving quickly to make meaningful connections—prioritizing action and then using empathetic listening and alignment to deepen those connections. This chapter will introduce Responsive Resonance, define its core components, and provide insights into why it's so powerful in today's sales environment.

Responsive Resonance: An Overview

Responsive Resonance is, at its core, a combination of two ideas:

- **"Execute, then Think":** Taking immediate, decisive action to begin a conversation or start building a relationship.
- **"Relational Resonance":** Transitioning from action to empathy-driven engagement, focusing on aligning with the client's tone, energy, and needs to foster an authentic connection.

Together, these approaches enable sales professionals to make swift, intentional contact without getting bogged down by over-preparation, and then to build on that contact by tuning into the client's personality and preferences. This mix of immediacy and adaptability allows for quicker, more effective relationships that evolve naturally rather than feeling forced or formulaic.

The Purpose of Responsive Resonance

Responsive Resonance was designed to address the following challenges that many sales professionals face today:

1. **Breaking Through the Noise:** In a crowded marketplace, being quick and authentic can set you apart. Clients are inundated with emails, calls, and messages daily; those that cut through are often those that feel genuine, spontaneous, and in tune with the client's needs.
2. **Balancing Speed and Authenticity:** Many sales strategies focus on one or the other—fast action or deep connection. Responsive Resonance brings both together, allowing you to act quickly while ensuring every interaction feels personal and considerate.
3. **Creating Lasting Connections:** Rather than chasing a quick "yes," Responsive Resonance aims to build relationships that lead to long-term partnerships. The goal is to establish trust and alignment from the very beginning, resulting in higher-quality leads and better retention.

How Responsive Resonance Works

Responsive Resonance is broken down into four core steps, each of which we'll explore in more detail in later chapters:

1. **Quick Initiation:** Start by taking immediate action—whether it's a call, message, or spontaneous conversation. Don't wait for the perfect moment; just begin.
2. **Resonant Engagement:** Once you've initiated contact, shift to a more energy-focused, relational approach. Listen closely, attune to the client's tone, and mirror their style to build rapport quickly.
3. **Momentum Maintenance:** Keep the relationship alive through timely, thoughtful follow-ups. These follow-ups should feel light, adding value without pressure.
4. **Natural Close and Deeper Commitment:** Rather than pushing for an instant "yes," use the foundation you've built to suggest logical next steps. This leads to a commitment that feels authentic and mutual.

The Relevance of Responsive Resonance in Today's Sales Environment

In a world where clients are increasingly seeking brands and professionals they can trust, Responsive Resonance is more relevant than ever. Here's why:

1. **Trust as a Differentiator:** Clients value trust as much as they value product quality or service. By starting with quick, authentic actions, you can demonstrate genuine interest without making the client feel like they're just a number.
2. **The Demand for Personalized Engagement:** Today's clients expect personalization. By adapting your style to each client's unique energy and preferences, you make every interaction feel personal and catered to them.
3. **The Need for Speed:** Fast decision-making is essential in competitive markets. Responsive Resonance allows you to engage quickly and adapt as you go, keeping up with clients' fast-paced expectations without compromising authenticity.

Case Study: The Power of "Execute, then Think"

Let's look at a real-world example of the "Execute, then Think" approach in action. Imagine a sales representative named Sarah, who was initially hesitant to reach out to a large potential client because she felt underprepared. Instead of waiting to gather more information, she decided to act on a gut feeling and sent a brief, friendly email introduction, offering a quick conversation.

The response was almost immediate, with the client expressing interest in learning more. By acting quickly and adapting to the client's tone and pace, Sarah was able to secure a first meeting and begin building rapport. This simple decision to act first and think later created an opportunity that otherwise might have been missed if she had waited.

Exercises

1. **Reflect on Your Sales Style:** Think about recent sales challenges where balancing quick action with genuine connection could have improved the outcome. Write down two or three examples.
2. **Case Study Review:** Examine a case study that shows the drawbacks of over-preparing versus the benefits of "Execute, then Think." Reflect on what you would have done differently in each scenario.
3. **Prepare for Quick Initiation:** Make a list of three potential clients you've been hesitant to reach out to. Draft a quick initiation message that feels authentic but isn't overly detailed or scripted.

Summary

Responsive Resonance combines the best of speed and empathy, making it possible to connect quickly and build genuine, lasting relationships. By embracing both the decisive action of “Execute, then Think” and the adaptive engagement of “Relational Resonance,” you can create client relationships that are meaningful, effective, and resilient in today’s sales landscape.

"If opportunity doesn't knock, build a door." –*Milton Berle*

Chapter 2: The Four Core Principles of Responsive Resonance

Introduction

The Responsive Resonance approach is built on four core principles that guide each stage of the sales process. These principles are designed to be flexible, allowing sales professionals to adapt to different clients, contexts, and challenges. In this chapter, we'll dive into each principle, exploring its purpose, techniques, and practical applications.

Principle 1: Initiate Instantly, Connect Meaningfully

Definition

This principle emphasizes the importance of starting strong and quickly. Whether you're reaching out via email, phone, or in person, the goal is to act without overthinking. By taking the first step quickly, you avoid the trap of analysis paralysis and create momentum.

How to Apply

1. **Start with Curiosity:** A curious mindset is often all you need to initiate a meaningful conversation. A friendly question or observation can break the ice naturally.
2. **Prioritize Action Over Perfection:** Rather than crafting a perfect script, focus on a clear, simple message that opens the door to engagement.
3. **Be Genuine and Direct:** Clients appreciate authenticity. Start with a brief, friendly message that conveys genuine interest and a willingness to help.

Example

Imagine you're reaching out to a potential client via email. Rather than writing a detailed proposal, try a short, friendly message:

"Hi [Client's Name], I noticed [personalized observation related to their business]. I'd love to connect briefly to learn more about your work and see if there's a way, we can support each other. Let me know if you're open to a quick chat!"

Practice Exercise

Write a simple outreach message for a new prospect. Focus on curiosity and authenticity, keeping the message under five sentences.

Principle 2: Align with Energy, Build Comfort Rapidly

Definition

Once you've made contact, shift into "Relational Resonance" mode. This means attuning to the client's energy, listening actively, and adapting your tone and style to match theirs.

How to Apply

1. **Listen Closely:** Pay attention to the client's words, tone, and body language. Are they reserved, energetic, formal, or casual?
2. **Mirror Their Style:** Subtly mirror their language and style without overdoing it. If they're formal, maintain a professional tone; if they're more relaxed, reflect that energy.
3. **Ask Open-Ended Questions:** Encourage them to share more about themselves by asking open-ended questions. This shows genuine interest and helps deepen the connection.

Example

If a client is speaking enthusiastically about a recent project, match their enthusiasm. You could say, "That sounds fantastic! What was your favorite part of the project?" This approach builds comfort by aligning with their excitement and showing genuine curiosity.

Practice Exercise

Think of a recent client conversation. How could you have better matched their energy? Write down two adjustments you could make next time to create more resonance.

Principle 3: Lead with Momentum, Adjust on the Fly

Definition

The third principle is about maintaining momentum while staying flexible. After initiating and aligning, keep the conversation flowing by adapting based on their responses and feedback.

How to Apply

1. **Stay Adaptable:** Be ready to change your approach based on the client's responses. If they seem hesitant, give them space; if they're engaged, dive deeper.
2. **Use Their Language:** If they use certain industry terms or phrases, mirror that language to show alignment and understanding.
3. **Don't Rush:** Instead of pushing for a quick agreement, take the time to fully explore their needs and ensure they feel comfortable.

Example

If a client mentions a challenge they're facing, use it as an opportunity to explore further. Ask questions that show understanding and avoid pushing your agenda prematurely.

Practice Exercise

Think of a situation where a client's response surprised you. How could you have adapted more effectively in real-time? Write down what you would do differently.

Principle 4: Turn Small Wins into Strong Foundations

Definition

Responsive Resonance encourages sales professionals to see every positive interaction as a small win that lays the groundwork for a deeper relationship. Each smile, nod, or positive response contributes to a growing foundation of trust.

How to Apply

1. **Celebrate Small Wins:** Recognize and appreciate small victories in each interaction, such as an enthusiastic response or a shared laugh.
2. **Build on Each Interaction:** Use each win as a steppingstone to deepen the relationship. Each follow-up should feel like a natural continuation of the last.
3. **Be Patient and Persistent:** Relationships take time to develop. Consistency is key, so stay in touch without overwhelming.

Example

After a positive initial call, follow up with a message that acknowledges the connection. For example, "It was great to connect today! I enjoyed hearing about [client's business or project], and I'm excited to see where we might work together."

Practice Exercise

Reflect on a recent client conversation. What was a "small win" you could celebrate? Write down a follow-up message that builds on that win.

Summary

The four principles of Responsive Resonance—**Initiate Instantly, Connect Meaningfully; Align with Energy, Build Comfort Rapidly; Lead with Momentum, adjust on the Fly;** and **Turn Small Wins into Strong Foundations**—create a strong foundation for authentic, adaptive sales relationships. These principles equip you with the tools to engage quickly, resonate deeply, and build partnerships that last.

In the next chapter, we'll explore the step-by-step process of Responsive Resonance, guiding you through each phase of initiating, deepening, maintaining, and closing client relationships with confidence and authenticity.

"Take risks: if you win, you will be happy; if you lose, you will be wise." – *Swami Vivekananda*

Chapter 3: The Step-by-Step Process of Responsive Resonance

Introduction

Now that we've covered the core principles, it's time to delve into the specific steps of the Responsive Resonance process. This chapter will provide a structured, step-by-step approach to using Responsive Resonance in every client interaction. This process is adaptable, meaning it can be customized to suit different types of clients and varying sales contexts.

Responsive Resonance is structured into four sequential steps: **Quick Initiation, Resonant Engagement, Maintaining Momentum,** and **Natural Close and Deeper Commitment.** Each step is designed to keep the interaction moving forward while building trust, understanding, and genuine rapport.

Step 1: Quick Initiation

Purpose:

To get the conversation started without overthinking. Quick Initiation helps break the inertia that can sometimes prevent sales interactions from happening at all.

Key Techniques:

1. **Start with Curiosity:** Use a question, observation, or relevant comment to pique the client's interest without making it feel scripted or rehearsed.
2. **Keep it Simple and Direct:** Initiate with a brief, friendly message that communicates interest without overwhelming details or a pushy tone. For example, a simple, "Hi [Name], I'd love to connect briefly to hear more about your business and see if there's a way we can help each other," can often be the perfect opener.
3. **Personalize When Possible:** Mention something specific to the client, such as a recent project they completed or an industry trend they might be interested in. This shows that you've done your homework and that you're reaching out with purpose.

Practical Example:

Imagine reaching out via LinkedIn. Rather than crafting a lengthy introduction, send a brief message like:

"Hi [Name], I saw your recent post about [relevant topic]. It sounds like an exciting area! I'd love to connect and hear more about your work."

This message shows interest, creates curiosity, and opens the door for further interaction without sounding overly formal or self-promotional.

Exercise:

Draft three different initiation messages for potential clients in your target industry. Keep each message under three sentences and focus on curiosity and friendliness. Then, practice sending these messages to real prospects.

Step 2: Resonant Engagement

Purpose:

Once contact is made, it's essential to move into an alignment phase, which we call **Resonant Engagement**. This step is about tuning into the client's energy and creating a comfortable, trust-based environment.

Key Techniques:

1. **Listen Actively:** Pay close attention to both what the client says and how they say it. Note their tone, body language (if in person or video call), and any expressions of enthusiasm or concern. Respond with questions that invite them to elaborate.
2. **Mirror Their Style and Language:** Subtly adjust your tone and language to reflect the client's style. If they're formal, match their tone. If they're conversational, feel free to use a more relaxed approach.
3. **Encourage Openness Through Questions:** Ask open-ended questions to show genuine interest and prompt the client to share more about their needs, challenges, or goals. This creates a two-way conversation rather than a one-sided pitch.

Practical Example:

If a client mentions a specific goal they're excited about, acknowledge it and ask a follow-up question. For example, "That sounds like a fantastic project! What are some of the biggest challenges you're working to overcome?" This question signals that you're genuinely interested in their work and committed to understanding their situation.

Exercise:

Think of a recent interaction where you could have aligned more closely with the client's style. Write down two adjustments you would make next time to improve Resonant Engagement. Practice these adjustments in your next client conversation.

Step 3: Maintaining Momentum

Purpose:

Once you've initiated contact and built rapport, the goal is to keep the relationship alive by consistently adding value. Maintaining Momentum involves thoughtful, well-timed follow-ups that engage the client without overwhelming them. Each follow-up should be intentional and aligned with the client's needs, reinforcing your commitment to their success. By staying responsive and providing relevant insights, you position yourself as a valuable partner rather than just a salesperson. This balance of persistence and sensitivity keeps the relationship fresh, deepens trust, and ensures the client feels supported over time.

Key Techniques:

1. **Timely Follow-Ups:** Send a follow-up message within 24–48 hours of your initial interaction. This could be a simple "Thanks for the great conversation!" or a message sharing relevant information or resources based on what you discussed.
2. **Add Value, Don't Push:** Every follow-up should feel beneficial rather than promotional. Share articles, insights, or resources that align with the client's interests or goals.
3. **Keep the Conversation Light and Friendly:** Avoid heavy-handed asks. Instead, focus on keeping the conversation friendly and curiosity-driven until the client is ready to take things to the next level.

Practical Example:

Imagine you had an initial call with a client who mentioned they're interested in sustainable practices. A few days later, you might follow up with an article on recent trends in sustainability relevant to their industry. A message could look like this:

"Hi [Name], I came across this article on sustainability practices in [industry] and thought you might find it interesting. Hope all is well!"

This follow-up adds value and keeps the conversation active without pressuring the client.

Exercise:

Develop a follow-up strategy for three different clients. For each one, outline the timing and content of your follow-ups, focusing on how you can add value with each interaction.

Step 4: Natural Close and Deeper Commitment

Purpose:
The closing phase in Responsive Resonance is about advancing the relationship in a way that feels natural and mutually beneficial. By positioning the next steps as a logical progression rather than a hard sell, you reinforce the trust and alignment you've carefully established. This approach invites the client to view the decision as collaborative, encouraging them to take action based on shared goals rather than feeling pressured. Each suggestion is rooted in their specific needs and preferences, making the close feel like an organic next step that supports their objectives. Ultimately, this method transforms the closing phase into a confirmation of partnership, emphasizing long-term value over a quick transaction.

Key Techniques:

1. **Position the Next Step as a Natural Progression:** Use the client's words and goals as a foundation for your suggestion. Frame the next step as a mutually beneficial choice that aligns with their needs.
2. **Avoid Pressure, Reinforce Trust:** Instead of trying to seal the deal, use a soft close approach that respects the client's pace. This could mean suggesting a product demo, another conversation, or even a limited trial.
3. **Confirm Mutual Value:** Emphasize how the proposed next step benefits both sides. For example, "I think a demo would give us a chance to see if this is the right fit for your goals."

Practical Example:

After a series of positive interactions, propose a next step in a way that respects the client's pace:

"Based on our conversations, it sounds like [Solution/Product] could be a great fit for your goals. Would you be open to a quick demo to explore it further?"

This message is non-intrusive, and it aligns with the rapport you've built, positioning the close as a shared decision.

Exercise:

Practice crafting soft-close messages for different scenarios. Focus on language that feels respectful and collaborative and be prepared to adjust based on the client's response.

Summary

The Responsive Resonance process—Quick Initiation, Resonant Engagement, Maintaining Momentum, and Natural Close and Deeper Commitment—gives you a structured yet flexible framework for building connections. This process enables you to act quickly, establish rapport, and deepen relationships, leading to partnerships that feel both genuine and productive.

"Opportunities don't happen. You create them." – *Chris Grosser*

Chapter 4: Quick Initiation – Building Momentum Fast

Introduction

Quick Initiation is the first step in Responsive Resonance. The goal here is to open the door to conversation without getting bogged down in planning. Many sales professionals overthink the opening step, trying to craft the perfect email or call script. Quick Initiation is about shifting from perfectionism to immediacy, starting strong, and creating momentum that can carry the interaction forward.

The Mindset of Quick Initiation

Quick Initiation requires a shift in mindset. Rather than waiting for the perfect moment or crafting the ideal pitch, it's about starting with what you know and making the best of it. Here are a few perspectives to adopt:

1. **Focus on Curiosity Over Perfection:** Rather than approaching with a rigid plan, enter with genuine curiosity. Curiosity-driven outreach feels more natural and invites the client to share.
2. **Accept Imperfection:** Imperfection is often more relatable than perfection. A quick, genuine message often resonates better than a polished but impersonal one.
3. **Trust Your Instincts:** Use your intuition to guide you. Sales professionals who trust their instincts tend to make more authentic connections.

How to Apply Quick Initiation

1. **Use Simple, Direct Language:** Keep your message straightforward. Instead of a long introduction, open with a brief, friendly line that makes the client feel seen and valued.
2. **Include a Relevant Detail:** Reference something specific about the client to show that your outreach is intentional. This could be a recent project, a shared industry, or a mutual connection.
3. **End with an Open Invitation:**Rather than pushing for a meeting, keep it light and open. For instance, "I'd love to connect briefly if you're open to it" feels more comfortable than asking for a 30-minute call immediately.

Practical Examples of Quick Initiation

Example 1: LinkedIn Outreach

"Hi [Name], I saw your post about [topic]. It sounds like a fascinating area! I'd love to connect and learn more about your work."

This message is short, direct, and conveys genuine interest.

Example 2: Email Introduction

"Hi [Name], I noticed [specific detail about the client's work]. I thought it would be great to connect and explore how we might support each other. Let me know if you're open to a quick chat!"

This email uses a relevant detail to show authenticity and keeps the ask low-pressure.

Quick Initiation Practice Exercise

1. Write three different initiation messages for a potential client, using curiosity and friendliness as your guides.
2. Reach out to real prospects using these messages, paying attention to how the clients respond.

"Don't be afraid to give up the good to go for the great." – ***John D. Rockefeller***

Chapter 5: Resonant Engagement – Deepening the Connection

Introduction

Resonant Engagement is the second step in Responsive Resonance, where you move from initiating contact to deepening the connection. This step is about creating comfort and trust by aligning with the client's energy. Resonant Engagement requires active listening, subtle mirroring, and a natural curiosity that helps the client feel understood and valued.

The Purpose of Resonant Engagement

The goal of Resonant Engagement is to build rapport and make the client feel comfortable. When clients feel at ease, they're more likely to open up about their goals, challenges, and needs. This step is where you start laying the foundation for a long-term relationship based on mutual respect and understanding.

How to Apply Resonant Engagement

1. **Listen Actively:** Pay close attention to both what the client says and how they say it. Notice their tone, pace, and enthusiasm.
2. **Mirror Their Style:** If the client is formal, maintain a professional tone. If they're more casual, match their relaxed style. This mirroring creates subtle resonance and makes the conversation feel more natural.
3. **Ask Open-Ended Questions:** Use questions that invite the client to share more about themselves. Avoid yes-or-no questions; instead, ask about their challenges, goals, or preferences.

Practical Techniques for Resonant Engagement

Technique 1: Pacing and Tone Matching

Match the client's pace and tone as closely as possible. If they're speaking quickly, stay engaged and responsive. If they're speaking slowly or thoughtfully, adopt a more reflective tone.

Technique 2: Empathetic Listening

Show understanding through verbal acknowledgments, such as, "I understand," or "That makes sense." These responses reinforce that you're truly listening and respect their input.

Technique 3: Thoughtful Questioning

Ask questions that demonstrate a deep interest in their experience and insights. For example, "What inspired you to focus on [project or goal]?" This approach signals genuine curiosity.

Resonant Engagement Practice Exercise

1. Think of a recent conversation where you could have used better alignment. Write down two adjustments you would make to improve engagement.
2. Practice these adjustments in your next client conversation.

Summary

Quick Initiation and Resonant Engagement are the foundational steps of Responsive Resonance. Quick Initiation breaks the ice, while Resonant Engagement creates comfort and deepens the connection. By combining decisive action with empathy, these steps enable you to form meaningful relationships that feel both natural and effective.

In the next chapter, we'll discuss how to maintain the momentum you've created, keeping the engagement alive with timely follow-ups that add value without overwhelming the client.

"The first step towards getting somewhere is to decide you're not going to stay where you are." – J.P. Morgan

Chapter 6: Maintaining Momentum and Curiosity

Introduction

You've made initial contact, aligned with the client's energy, and established rapport. Now comes a crucial phase of the Responsive Resonance approach: maintaining the momentum. This chapter focuses on the art of follow-up and value-adding, allowing you to keep the relationship alive without overwhelming the client. By staying engaged in a way that feels natural and valuable, you build anticipation, curiosity, and a growing sense of trust. Momentum maintenance is about staying connected, remaining relevant, and adding layers of value, so the client feels supported and understood.

In this chapter, you'll learn how to keep clients interested by creating touchpoints that add value and inspire curiosity, deepening the connection you've established.

The Purpose of Maintaining Momentum

Maintaining momentum is essential to ensure that initial enthusiasm doesn't fade into disinterest. This step creates a "drip effect" of value over time, allowing clients to see your continued investment in their needs. By staying engaged without pressuring them, you reinforce trust and position yourself as a partner rather than just a salesperson.

The goal here is to keep the client engaged at a comfortable pace, adding value without overwhelming them or rushing for an immediate sale. Each touchpoint should be light, friendly, and focused on building rapport while subtly reinforcing your value.

Key Techniques for Maintaining Momentum

1. **Timely Follow-Ups**: A timely follow-up shows attentiveness and respect for the client's time. Ideally, a follow-up should be made within 24–48 hours after your initial conversation. Whether you're following up on a previous conversation, sharing a helpful resource, or simply checking in, this small gesture makes a big impact.

2. **Add Value with Each Touchpoint**: Ensure that every follow-up offers something of value, such as an article, resource, or insight related to the client's interests. Adding value at each step demonstrates your commitment to understanding their needs and making their lives easier.

3. **Use Light, Curiosity-Driven Language:** Keep the tone light and curiosity-driven. Instead of pushing for a commitment, express genuine interest in their progress or challenges. This helps keep the conversation comfortable and friendly, encouraging the client to share openly.

4. **Respect Their Space and Timing**: Be mindful of the client's responses and adjust your timing accordingly. If they're slow to respond, allow some breathing room before following up again. This respect for their space shows empathy and builds trust.

Examples of Maintaining Momentum

Example 1: Sharing an article or Resource

Imagine you had a positive call with a client who mentioned their focus on a specific challenge, such as digital transformation. A few days later, send them a relevant article or resource:

"Hi [Client's Name], I came across this article on digital transformation in [industry] and thought you might find it interesting! Let me know if it resonates with what you're working on."

This approach keeps the connection alive and offers value without any push for action.

Example 2: Checking in After a Previous Conversation

If your last conversation ended on a high note, follow up with a friendly check-in a week later:

"Hi [Client's Name], just wanted to see how things are going with [project or challenge discussed]. No rush on my end—just here to support if you need anything!"

This light, open-ended check-in keeps the lines of communication open while showing that you're invested in their success.

Best Practices for Follow-Ups and Value-Adding

1. **Personalize Where Possible**

   Tailor each follow-up to reflect something specific about the client's business, goals, or interests. This can be as simple as referencing a recent project they're working on or addressing a challenge they mentioned in your last conversation.

2.

3. **Aim for Consistency, Not Frequency**

   Momentum doesn't mean contacting them constantly. Instead, it's about staying top of mind without being overbearing. A consistent, well-timed follow-up every week or two can be more effective than multiple follow-ups in a short period.

4.

5. **Offer Help, Don't Push for Decisions**

6. Rather than asking if they're ready to move forward, offer assistance and reinforce your availability to support them. Statements like, "Let me know how I can help with [specific need]" feel more supportive than transactional.

Practical Exercises for Maintaining Momentum

1. **Create a Follow-Up Strategy for Three Clients**

   Choose three current or potential clients and map out a 2–3-week follow-up plan for each. For each touchpoint, identify what value you'll offer and how you'll personalize the message to maintain engagement without pressure.

2.
3. **Draft Value-Adding Messages**

   Practice drafting three different types of follow-up messages: one that shares a resource, one that checks in after a previous conversation, and one that offers specific assistance. Focus on keeping the tone friendly, supportive, and non-transactional.

4. **Set a Follow-Up Reminder**
5.

   Use a calendar or CRM tool to set a follow-up reminder after each client interaction. This ensures you stay consistent with your follow-ups, making it easier to maintain momentum over time.

Summary

Maintaining momentum is an art that requires consistency, empathy, and a commitment to adding value. By keeping touchpoints light, timely, and valuable, you build trust and deepen the client relationship without overwhelming them. This phase is where relationships transition from "initial interest" to "genuine connection," setting the stage for a natural close.

In the next chapter, we'll explore how to bring the relationship to the next level with techniques for a **Natural Close and Deeper Commitment** that feel organic and mutually beneficial.

"**Start where you are. Use what you have. Do what you can.**" – *Arthur Ashe*

Chapter 7: Natural Closing Techniques

Introduction

Closing a sale doesn't have to feel like a hard sell. In fact, with Responsive Resonance, closing is a natural progression that emerges from the rapport, trust, and value you've established. The aim is to suggest the next steps in a way that feels comfortable and supportive, inviting the client to move forward rather than pressuring them to commit. This chapter will guide you through techniques for a **Natural Close**—an approach to closing that focuses on reinforcing the relationship and mutual benefits, rather than rushing to a decision.

The Purpose of a Natural Close

A natural close prioritizes relationship depth and alignment. Rather than making the client feel pushed, this approach encourages them to see the next step as a logical and beneficial choice. By positioning the close as a mutual decision based on shared understanding, you can achieve a commitment that feels positive for both sides.

A natural close leverages everything you've established in previous steps. The trust built in Resonant Engagement and the momentum maintained through follow-ups come together to make the close feel comfortable and logical, making the client feel ready to take the next step with confidence.

Key Techniques for a Natural Close

1. **Suggest a Next Step as a Partnership:** Rather than framing the close as a sale, present it as a collaborative step that benefits both sides. For example, propose a demo, trial, or consultation that aligns with their needs.

2. **Use Their Language to Reinforce Alignment:** Reflect back any language the client has used about their goals or challenges. This makes it clear that the next step is designed with their best interests in mind and shows that you're listening.

3. **Invite, Don't Pressure:** Instead of asking for a definitive "yes," invite the client to explore the next step. Phrasing like, "Would you be open to discussing this further?" feels softer and more collaborative.

4. **Offer a Clear but Flexible Commitment:** While you want to encourage a decision, keep the options flexible. For instance, if you're suggesting a trial, keep the timeframe open. This shows you're focused on their comfort rather than rushing them

Examples of Natural Closing Techniques

Example 1: Soft Close for a Demo or Trial

If a client has shown interest but hasn't fully committed, suggest a low-pressure next step:
"Based on our conversations, it sounds like [Solution/Product] could really support your goals. How about we do a quick demo to see if it's a fit?"
This phrasing is inviting and focused on helping them, positioning the demo as a way to explore options without obligation.

Example 2: Alignment Close for Service Offerings

For service-based solutions, frame the close as a logical progression that aligns with their needs:

"It sounds like our consulting services could be a great fit for the project you described. Would you be open to a brief strategy session to discuss how we might support your goals?"

This language reinforces alignment and invites the client to explore without immediate pressure.

Best Practices for the Natural Close

1. **Reinforce Shared Goals and Benefits**
   Remind the client of how your product or service aligns with their goals. Using statements like, "This could really support the work you're already doing" helps them see the close as a beneficial choice.
2. **Respect Their Timing and Preferences**
   Be mindful of any hints the client has given about their timeline or pace. If they've mentioned needing more time, offer a flexible commitment or follow-up.
3. **Follow Up After the Close**
   Even after the client agrees to the next step, continue to follow up with support and guidance. This reinforces the relationship and builds confidence in the commitment they've made.

Practical Exercises for the Natural Close

1. **Craft Three Closing Messages**

   Write three closing messages for different scenarios—a demo offer, a trial offer, and a consultation. Focus on using language that feels natural and collaborative.

2. **Practice with a Partner**

   Partner with a colleague or friend and practice delivering your closing messages. Pay attention to tone, pace, and comfort. Ask for feedback on whether the close feels natural and supportive.

3. **Follow-Up Preparation**

   Plan a follow-up message for after a successful close. This message should reinforce the decision, offer support, and keep the relationship strong.

Summary

A Natural Close is the culmination of the trust, rapport, and momentum you've established. By positioning the close as, a collaborative step aligned with the client's goals, you create a commitment that feels positive and mutually beneficial. This approach makes the close feel like a natural outcome rather than a sales tactic, leading to long-term partnerships built on trust and shared objectives.

With a solid understanding of Quick Initiation, Resonant Engagement, Maintaining Momentum, and the Natural Close, you now have the tools to use Responsive Resonance to its fullest. In the following chapters, we'll explore advanced techniques for applying this method across different industries and client types, allowing you to adapt and refine your approach for maximum impact.

By combining light touchpoints, value-added engagement, and a natural closing approach, Chapters 6 and 7 provide readers with essential tools to keep clients engaged and ready to commit without feeling pressured. These techniques ensure that the entire sales process feels as authentic and mutually beneficial as possible.

"Dream big and dare to fail." – Norman Vaughan

Chapter 8: Communication Best Practices

Introduction

Communication is the foundation of Responsive Resonance. Each interaction—whether it's a first outreach, a follow-up, or a closing conversation—relies on effective, adaptive communication to build trust and keep the relationship moving forward. This chapter will provide essential communication techniques for each stage of Responsive Resonance, giving you the tools to make every message resonate.

In this chapter, we'll cover practical language tips, tone adjustments, and phrasing templates that help you navigate client interactions with ease. With these best practices, you can adapt quickly to different personalities and situations, ensuring that every conversation feels natural, friendly, and effective.

Why Communication Matters in Responsive Resonance

In the Responsive Resonance model, communication is not only about what you say but also about how you say it. The right phrasing, tone, and timing create a sense of comfort and trust, helping clients feel valued and understood. Good communication builds rapport, while poor communication can cause disconnection or even push the client away.

Effective communication does the following:

1. **Conveys Empathy and Understanding:** When you use language that reflects a client's needs and emotions, they feel understood and valued.
2. **Establishes Clarity and Confidence:** Clear, confident language helps clients feel assured in their decisions. This is particularly important in sales, where clients need to trust that they're making the right choice.
3. **Keeps the Relationship Fluid and Engaging:** By adapting your tone and approach, you can keep the conversation fresh, friendly, and engaging, allowing the relationship to grow naturally over time.

Best Practices for Communication in Each Step of Responsive Resonance

Step 1: Quick Initiation

The language used in the Quick Initiation phase should be simple, direct, and genuine. Avoid overly formal language or elaborate phrasing, as these can create distance. Instead, focus on sparking curiosity and opening the door to connection.

Quick Initiation Phrasing Examples:

- "Hi [Name], I noticed your work in [specific area]. It sounds interesting, and I'd love to connect and learn more."
- "Hello [Name], I came across your profile and thought it would be great to connect. Let me know if you're open to a quick chat."

Key Tips:

1. **Use Simple, Concise Language:** A clear, straightforward approach feels genuine and approachable.
2. **Convey Curiosity:**Phrasing that invites the client to share creates openness and builds rapport.

Step 2: Resonant Engagement

Once the connection is established, shift to a more client-centered tone. Resonant Engagement requires active listening and an alignment with the client's style and language. Use language that reflects their interests, needs, and goals, showing them that you're genuinely interested in their situation.

Resonant Engagement Phrasing Examples:

- "I appreciate you sharing that; it sounds like a fascinating project. What are some of the biggest challenges you're facing with it?"
- "That sounds great! I'd love to hear more about how you got involved in [area of interest]."

Key Tips:

1. **Ask Open-Ended Questions:** Questions like "How did that go for you?" or "What do you think about [specific topic]?" encourage them to share.
2. **Match Their Language and Tone:** Notice if they're using industry-specific terms, formal language, or casual phrasing, and mirror their style.

Step 3: Maintaining Momentum

In this phase, your communication should remain light and valuable. The tone is supportive and friendly, without being overly persistent. Value-driven language keeps the client engaged and interested in continuing the relationship.

Maintaining Momentum Phrasing Examples:

- "Just thought you might enjoy this article on [topic they mentioned]. It aligns with what we discussed the other day."
- "I was thinking about our conversation and thought this resource might be useful for [specific need]. Let me know if you find it helpful!"

Key Tips:

1. **Provide Value, Not Pressure:** Offer information, resources, or assistance without pushing for a commitment.
2. **Use Language That Invites Curiosity:** Phrasing like, "I thought of you when I saw this," feels personal and considerate.

Step 4: Natural Close and Deeper Commitment

For a Natural Close, your language should focus on mutual benefits and shared goals.

The tone here is collaborative, making it clear that you're focused on finding a solution that truly aligns with their needs. Avoid aggressive or sales-heavy language and instead position the next step as a logical, beneficial progression.

Natural Close Phrasing Examples:

- "Based on our discussions, it sounds like [solution] would support your goals. Would you be open to exploring it further?"
- "I think we could create something really valuable here. Would you be interested in a brief demo to see if it's the right fit?"

Key Tips:

1. **Emphasize Alignment with Their Goals:** Reinforce that the next step is in their best interest and aligns with their needs.
2. **Invite Rather Than Push:**Use language that feels inviting, such as "explore further" or "consider," to keep the tone comfortable and respectful.

Additional Tips for Effective Communication

1. **Be Mindful of Timing**

   Respect the client's time by keeping messages concise and only reaching out during appropriate hours. Spacing out follow-ups also shows that you respect their space.
2. **Adapt Based on Feedback**

   If the client shows hesitation, be ready to shift your approach. Use softer language, give them space, and be mindful of non-verbal cues if you're speaking in person or on video.
3. **Stay Positive and Supportive**

   Language that feels positive and solution-focused reassures the client that you're committed to their success. For instance, instead of saying, "I understand that's challenging," say, "I'd love to help make this easier for you."

Practical Exercises for Improving Communication

1. **Phrase Practice:** Create three different responses for each stage of Responsive Resonance. Focus on adapting the phrasing for different personalities (e.g., formal, casual, reserved, or energetic).

2. Tone Matching Exercise: Practice matching your tone to different styles—formal, conversational, empathetic, etc. Record yourself, if possible, to listen back and refine your approach.

3. Feedback Loop: Practice with a colleague or friend and ask for feedback on how your tone and language come across. Are you sounding genuine, supportive, and aligned with their needs?

Summary

Effective communication is the thread that connects each phase of Responsive Resonance. By adjusting your language, tone, and timing, you can make every interaction feel personalized and meaningful. The best communicators know how to align with their clients in a way that fosters trust and encourages open, honest conversation.

In the next chapter, we'll explore how to apply Responsive Resonance to a variety of real-world sales scenarios, adapting the approach to different industries, client types, and situations for maximum impact.

"Life begins at the end of your comfort zone." – Neale Donald Walsch

Chapter 9: Applying Responsive Resonance to Real-World Scenarios

Introduction

Responsive Resonance is a versatile approach that can be adapted across different industries, client types, and sales contexts. This chapter will show you how to apply the Responsive Resonance framework to real-world scenarios, allowing you to customize your approach based on client needs and preferences. Whether you're in B2B, B2C, tech, consulting, or service industries, Responsive Resonance can be tailored to resonate with each unique client and situation.

Adapting Responsive Resonance to Different Industries

Each industry has its own nuances, and the way you apply Responsive Resonance should reflect those differences. Below are some common industries and tips for customizing your approach in each.

1. B2B Sales

B2B clients often focus on data, ROI, and long-term impact. In B2B, building trust and understanding their strategic goals is key.

Adaptation Tips:

- **Focus on Long-Term Value:** Emphasize the lasting benefits of your solution and how it aligns with their business strategy.
- **Use Data to Support Your Points:** Share relevant case studies, data, or research that backs up your claims and shows measurable outcomes.
- **Offer Strategic Insights:** Position yourself as a partner who can help achieve their goals, not just a salesperson.

2. B2C Sales

In B2C, the focus is more on personal benefits and emotional appeal. B2C clients are often looking for products or services that simplify their lives or enhance their personal satisfaction.

Adaptation Tips:

- **Emphasize Immediate Benefits:** Focus on how your product or service can make their life easier or more enjoyable right now.
- **Build a Relatable Connection:** Show empathy and understanding of their personal needs or lifestyle preferences.
- **Use Visuals and Demonstrations:** B2C clients respond well to visuals, so share demos, images, or testimonials that help them envision the experience.

3. Tech Sales

In tech, clients are often focused on innovation, efficiency, and scalability. Tech clients want to know that a product is cutting-edge and can adapt to future needs.

Adaptation Tips:

Highlight Innovation and Flexibility: Emphasize the latest features, adaptability, and how your solution can grow with them.

Speak to Technical Benefits: Be prepared to discuss technical details and performance. Showing a solid understanding of tech specifications builds credibility.

Offer Demos and Trials: Tech clients often need hands-on experience, so offer demos or trial periods to help them experience the value firsthand.

Adapting Responsive Resonance to Different Client Types

Not all clients are the same; some are more analytical, others more intuitive or relational. Here's how to adjust your approach based on different client personalities.

1. Analytical Clients

Analytical clients tend to focus on data, facts, and logic. They prefer detailed information and appreciate thorough explanations.

Adaptation Tips:

Provide Detailed Information: Share reports, case studies, and any quantifiable results.

Use Logical Phrasing: Avoid vague language and be as specific as possible when discussing benefits.

Be **Patient and Methodical:** Allow them time to think through their decisions and be prepared to answer detailed questions.

2. Relational Clients

Relational clients value personal connection and are more likely to make decisions based on trust and rapport.

Adaptation Tips:

- **Focus on Building Rapport:** Spend extra time establishing a personal connection. They're more likely to buy from someone they feel comfortable with.
- **Use Empathetic Language:** Show that you understand their concerns and priorities.
- **Reinforce Mutual Goals:** Emphasize shared values and goals, framing the relationship as a partnership.

3. Intuitive Clients

Intuitive clients often make decisions based on gut feeling or a sense of alignment. They respond well to open-ended, conversational approaches.

Adaptation Tips:

- **Encourage Open Conversation:** Give them space to express themselves and discuss their thoughts.
- **Use Storytelling:** They respond well to stories and examples that illustrate how your solution has helped others.
- **Avoid Overloading with Details:** Keep the conversation focused on the big picture rather than the specifics.

Applying Responsive Resonance in Common Sales Scenarios

Responsive Resonance can also be adapted to specific sales situations, such as cold calls, presentations, and follow-ups. Here's how to apply it in three common scenarios.

Scenario 1: Cold Calls

In a cold call, the goal is to make a quick connection and establish interest without overwhelming the prospect.

Tips for Cold Calls:

- **Start with a Quick Introduction:** Keep it simple and mention something specific about the client's industry or needs.
- **Ask Open-Ended Questions Early:** This shows interest and allows them to share, giving your insight into their needs.
- **Respect Their Time:** Be concise and ask if they're available to continue the conversation, giving them a sense of control.

Scenario 2: Presentations

When presenting to a group, you need to balance personalization with clear, structured messaging.

Tips for Presentations:

- **Start with Their Goals:** Tailor the opening to address their specific goals or challenges.
- **Use Visuals and Data:** Engage both visual and analytical clients by incorporating data, graphs, and visuals that reinforce your points.
- **Invitation Questions:** Allow room for questions throughout to make the presentation feel interactive and responsive.

Scenario 3: Follow-Ups

Follow-ups should be personalized and light, with a focus on maintaining the momentum of the relationship.

Tips for Follow-Ups:

- **Keep it Friendly and Relevant:** Use a tone that feels like a casual check-in rather than a hard push.
- **Provide Value with Each Follow-Up:** Share a new insight or update that might interest them based on previous conversations.
- **Respect Their Response Rate:** If they take time to respond, adjust your follow-up frequency accordingly.

Practical Exercises for Applying Responsive Resonance in Real-World Scenarios

1. **Industry-Specific Scenario:** Practice Choose an industry you work in or want to focus on and write down three ways you would adapt Responsive Resonance to meet the needs of that industry's clients.

2. **Client Type Role-Playing:** Practice role-playing conversations with each of the three client types (analytical, relational, intuitive). Focus on adjusting your language, tone, and approach for each type.

3. **Scenario Adaptation:** Select a specific sales scenario (e.g., cold call, presentation, follow-up) and write a full script that applies Responsive Resonance principles. Practice delivering the script to ensure it feels natural and adaptable.

Summary

Responsive Resonance is versatile and can be customized to fit different industries, client types, and sales scenarios. By adapting your approach to the context, you can build stronger, more effective relationships that meet the unique needs of each client. This adaptability is what makes Responsive Resonance such a powerful tool for modern sales professionals—it empowers you to meet clients where they are, in ways that feel both natural and impactful.

In the final chapter, we'll cover how to evaluate your progress and refine your personal style within the Responsive Resonance framework, ensuring continuous improvement and mastery over time.

"The future belongs to those who believe in the beauty of their dreams." – Eleanor Roosevelt

Chapter 10: Evaluating Your Progress and Refining Your Style

Introduction

Mastery of Responsive Resonance doesn't happen overnight. Like any skill, it requires practice, reflection, and continuous improvement. This final chapter will guide you through evaluating your progress, setting measurable goals, and refining your unique style within the Responsive Resonance framework. The goal is not only to track success but also to identify areas where you can grow, allowing you to adapt and enhance your approach over time.

Evaluating your progress means looking at more than just sales numbers; it involves assessing the quality of your client relationships, the effectiveness of your communication, and your ability to adapt to different scenarios. By focusing on both quantitative and qualitative measures, you can gain a full picture of your growth and make adjustments that will lead to even greater success.

Why Evaluating Progress Matters

Responsive Resonance is about more than closing deals—it's about building connections and creating value. Regularly evaluating your performance allows you to:

1. **Identify Strengths and Weaknesses:** Understanding where you excel and where you need improvement lets you focus on making targeted adjustments.
2. **Set Clear, Achievable Goals:** Defining specific goals within the Responsive Resonance framework gives you milestones to work toward, keeping you motivated and focused.
3. **Ensure Continuous Improvement:** Sales is a dynamic field, and clients need change over time. Regular evaluation helps you stay adaptable, fine-tuning your style to align with evolving client expectations.
4. **Strengthen Authenticity and Comfort in Your Style:**By assessing your approach, you can identify what feels most natural and effective for you, leading to a style that is both authentic and comfortable.

How to Evaluate Your Progress in Responsive Resonance

Effective evaluation involves setting key performance indicators (KPIs), seeking feedback, and engaging in regular self-reflection. Here's how to structure your evaluation:

1. Set Key Performance Indicators (KPIs) Aligned with Responsive Resonance

KPIs should reflect both the results and the process of Responsive Resonance. Consider setting KPIs in three main areas:

- **Connection KPIs:** These measure your ability to initiate and establish rapport quickly. Examples include the number of initial meetings secured, positive responses from outreach, or time taken to establish rapport.
- **Engagement KPIs:** These measure the quality of your engagement. Track things like client feedback, engagement scores from follow-ups, or the percentage of clients moving from initial contact to engaged conversations.
- **Closing KPIs:** These measure your ability to bring conversations to a natural, mutually beneficial close. Metrics might include conversion rate, client retention rate, and follow-up responses post-close.

2. Request Feedback from Clients and Peers

Client feedback provides insight into how your style resonates with others. For example, if clients feel comfortable and supported throughout the process, you're likely achieving the intended impact of Responsive Resonance. Consider occasional feedback requests to understand your clients' experiences.

Peer feedback is also valuable. Colleagues and mentors can offer fresh perspectives and may notice areas where you could improve. Regular check-ins or debriefs with a trusted peer can help you refine your approach.

3. Conduct Regular Self-Reflection

Set aside time each week or month to reflect on your recent interactions. Ask yourself:

> **What worked well in my recent conversations?**
> **Where did I struggle to maintain resonance with the client?**
> **What feedback or signals did I miss, and how could I handle it better next time?**
> **Which principles of Responsive Resonance felt most natural, and which felt challenging?**

Self-reflection allows you to turn each interaction into a learning opportunity, making continuous improvement a natural part of your routine.

Refining Your Personal Style

Responsive Resonance is flexible, allowing for personal adaptation based on your strengths and personality. Refining your style involves identifying which elements of Responsive Resonance resonate most with you and tailoring them to suit your authentic approach.

1. Identify Your Natural Strengths

Consider which parts of Responsive Resonance you find easiest and most enjoyable. Maybe you're particularly skilled at Quick Initiation, or you excel at creating alignment in Resonant Engagement. Focusing on these strengths can help you refine your approach while maintaining authenticity.

2. Experiment with Different Techniques

Try adjusting elements of your style to see what feels most effective. For example:

- **Adjust Your Language:** Experiment with different types of phrasing in each phase. If formal language feels forced, try a more conversational tone. If casual language doesn't resonate, try a more polished approach.
- **Vary Your Follow-Up Style:** Try different methods of maintaining momentum, such as voice messages, emails, or video messages, to see which gets the best response.
- **Explore Different Closing Techniques:** Experiment with soft-close phrases and approaches, finding which techniques feel most comfortable for both you and your clients.

3. Build on Your Authentic Communication Style

Clients are drawn to authenticity, so lean into what feels most genuine to you. The more comfortable you feel in your approach, the more likely clients will feel at ease, too. Authenticity strengthens your client relationships and enhances your reputation as someone clients can trust.

4. Adapt to Each Client's Unique Needs

Each client will respond differently to your approach, so refine your style based on their responses.

For instance, if you notice a client responds well to data, integrate more information into future conversations. If they respond better to empathy and storytelling, adjust your approach accordingly.

5. Continue Learning and Growing

Responsive Resonance is a skill that deepens with experience. Look for opportunities to continue learning, whether it's by studying client psychology, exploring new sales methodologies, or practicing additional communication techniques. The more you expand your knowledge and skills, the more versatile and effective your personal style will become.

Practical Exercises for Evaluating Progress and Refining Style

1. Set Quarterly Goals and KPIs

Define specific goals for each quarter, aligning them with the Responsive Resonance framework. For example, you might set a goal to improve your initial response rate by 10% or increase the number of clients who move from engagement to a natural close.

2. Keep a Reflection Journal

Dedicate a journal to self-reflection on your client interactions. After each significant conversation, write down what went well, what could be improved, and any specific takeaways. This practice makes self-reflection a habit, enabling continuous learning.

3. Role-Playing with a Peer

Regularly practice with a peer, using role-playing to try out new techniques or refine your style. Have them play different types of clients, providing feedback on how you adapt and communicate in each scenario.

4. Review Feedback and Make Adjustments

Periodically review any client and peer feedback you've received. Look for patterns in the feedback to identify recurring strengths and weaknesses. Make small, targeted adjustments based on this feedback to ensure continuous improvement.

5. Revisit Your Authentic Style

Reflect on which elements of Responsive Resonance feel the most natural for you. Consider how you can further align your approach with your unique personality, strengths, and values. This could mean refining your tone, adjusting your language, or altering your follow-up style to be even more authentic.

Summary

Evaluating your progress and refining your style are the keys to mastering Responsive Resonance. By setting measurable goals, seeking feedback, and engaging in regular self-reflection, you create a path for continuous improvement that ensures every client interaction is as impactful as possible. Over time, your personal style within Responsive Resonance will evolve, becoming more comfortable, authentic, and effective.

Responsive Resonance is more than a sales technique; it's a journey toward creating meaningful, mutually beneficial relationships. By continuously evaluating your approach and staying committed to growth, you'll not only excel in your role but also enjoy the fulfillment of building genuine connections.

With Responsive Resonance as your foundation, you can approach each client with confidence, authenticity, and adaptability—ready to create value and build trust in every interaction.

Final Word

As we reach the end of *The Art of Fast, Authentic Connections & Trust*, it's evident that creating meaningful connections is both an art and a discipline. Responsive Resonance Theory teaches us that genuine, impactful relationships stem from courage, empathy, and a commitment to trust. In a world driven by efficiency, Dr. Pirro's approach serves as a reminder that speed does not have to sacrifice authenticity. Quite the opposite—by initiating connections swiftly and following through with genuine, empathetic engagement, we can cultivate partnerships that endure.

This book invites us to reconsider the role we play in each interaction. Instead of merely focusing on outcomes, Responsive Resonance encourages us to focus on the quality of the connection. It asks us to see each interaction as an opportunity to build something meaningful, to approach each engagement with purpose, and to let the principles of trust and authenticity guide every step.

As you close this book, remember that these strategies are more than techniques—they're commitments to a way of engaging with others that brings lasting value to all involved. Whether in business or beyond, the principles shared here offer a path to meaningful connection in every interaction. Responsive Resonance isn't just a theory; it's an invitation to elevate the way we relate, engage, and build trust in all aspects of life.

Reference Section

This section provides a list of references and recommended readings that support and expand upon the principles of Responsive Resonance. These resources cover topics in sales, psychology, communication, relationship-building, and personal development, offering deeper insights into the foundations and applications of the Responsive Resonance framework.

Books

1. **Dale Carnegie** - *How to Win Friends and Influence People*
   This classic guide to communication and relationship-building offers timeless advice on connecting with others through empathy and understanding, which aligns closely with the Responsive Resonance approach.
2. **Daniel H. Pink** - *To Sell is Human: The Surprising Truth About Moving Others*
   Pink's exploration of modern sales techniques emphasizes empathy, adaptability, and the importance of human connection in effective sales practices.
3. **Chris Voss** - *Never Split the Difference: Negotiating as If Your Life Depended on It*
   Voss, a former FBI hostage negotiator, shares strategies on building rapport and creating trust—skills that are essential to the Resonant Engagement phase of Responsive Resonance.
4. **Robert Cialdini** - *Influence: The Psychology of Persuasion*
   Cialdini's insights into human psychology and persuasive techniques provide a foundation for understanding how clients respond to different types of communication and engagement.

5. **Stephen Covey** - *The 7 Habits of Highly Effective People*
   Covey's framework for personal and interpersonal effectiveness includes principles of trust-building, proactive engagement, and mutual benefit that resonate with the Responsive Resonance approach.
6. **John C. Maxwell** - *Everyone Communicates, Few Connect: What the Most Effective People Do Differently*
   Maxwell's work on connection emphasizes the importance of aligning with others' energy, using language that resonates, and building meaningful relationships in professional and personal contexts.

Articles and Journals

1. **Adam Grant** - "The Power of Empathy in Sales"
   Harvard Business Review, 2017
   Grant discusses the role of empathy and emotional intelligence in successful sales, explaining how connecting with clients on a personal level leads to lasting results.
2. **Deborah Tannen** - "The Power of Talk: Who Gets Heard and Why"
   Harvard Business Review, 1995
   Tannen's article on communication styles and gender provides insights into tone-matching and adaptive communication, core components of the Resonant Engagement stage.
3. **Shelley E. Taylor and Jonathan D. Brown** - "Illusion and Well-Being: A Social Psychological Perspective on Mental Health"
   Psychological Bulletin, 1988
   This research explores how positive reinforcement, and constructive engagement can impact clients' willingness to connect and trust, relevant to maintaining momentum and engagement.

Web Resources

1. **MindTools** - "Empathy at Work: Developing Skills to Understand Other People"

   www.Mindtools.com

   This online resource offers practical tips for building empathy, understanding body language, and developing active listening skills, which are essential for Resonant Engagement.

2. **SalesHacker** - "The Art of the Soft Close: 7 Strategies for Sealing the Deal Without the Hard Sell"

   www.saleshacker.com

   An article that provides tips for soft closing techniques, reinforcing the Natural Close approach in Responsive Resonance by focusing on subtle, mutually beneficial next steps.

3. **Harvard Business Review** - "How to Build a Meaningful Connection in Just 5 Minutes"

   www.hbr.org

   A practical guide on creating meaningful connections quickly, echoing the Quick Initiation and Resonant Engagement steps in Responsive Resonance.

4. **Psychology Today** - "Understanding and Building Rapport with Clients"

   www.psychologytoday.com

   This article outlines techniques for building rapport and developing trust, providing insights into the mental aspects of client relationship-building.

Further Reading and Development

1. **Emotional Intelligence Resources** - Daniel Goleman's *Emotional Intelligence: Why It Can Matter More Than IQ*
   Goleman's foundational work on emotional intelligence provides strategies for understanding emotions in oneself and others, an essential skill in all stages of Responsive Resonance.
2. **Digital Communication and Client Engagement** - *The Challenger Sale: Taking Control of the Customer Conversation* by Matthew Dixon and Brent Adamson
   This book explores ways to engage clients effectively through digital communication and proactive conversation, essential skills for modern sales professionals.
3. **Listening and Adaptive Skills** - *Just Listen: Discover the Secret to Getting Through to Absolutely Anyone* by Mark Goulston
   Goulston's insights into active listening and empathy align closely with the Resonant Engagement step, emphasizing the importance of creating trust and open dialogue.
4. **Building Authentic Client Relationships** - *Give and Take: Why Helping Others Drives Our Success* by Adam Grant
   Grant's work on the importance of creating value for others highlights how building trust and

providing genuine support can lead to greater professional success, a foundational concept in Responsive Resonance.

1. **Adaptive Communication** - *The Art of Adaptive Communication: A Guide to Creative Strategies in Sales and Relationship Building* by Carol Ellis
   This guide provides techniques for adjusting language, tone, and approach to match client needs, supporting the adaptive communication strategies in Responsive Resonance.

References (APA 7th)

Baldoni, J. (2013). *The leader's guide to speaking with presence.* AMACOM.

Baldwin, M. W. (2007). *Interpersonal cognition.* Guilford Press.

Berry, L. L. (1995). Relationship marketing of services—Growing interest, emerging perspectives. *Journal of the Academy of Marketing Science, 23*(4), 236–245. https://doi.org/10.1177/009207039502300402

Blau, P. M. (1964). *Exchange and power in social life.* Wiley.

Burgoon, J. K., Buller, D. B., & Woodall, W. G. (2000). *Nonverbal communication: The unspoken dialogue* (2nd ed.). McGraw-Hill.

Burgoon, J. K., Dillman, L., & Stern, L. A. (1996). *Interpersonal adaptation: Dyadic interaction patterns.* Cambridge University Press.

Carnegie, D. (2012). *How to win friends and influence people.* Simon & Schuster.

Chartrand, T. L., & Bargh, J. A. (1999). The chameleon effect: The perception-behavior link and social interaction. *Journal of Personality and Social Psychology, 76*(6), 893–910. https://doi.org/10.1037/0022-3514.76.6.893

Cialdini, R. B. (2006). *Influence: The psychology of persuasion.* Collins.

Cohen, S., & Wills, T. A. (1985). Stress, social support, and the buffering hypothesis. *Psychological Bulletin, 98*(2), 310–357. https://doi.org/10.1037/0033-2909.98.2.310

Covey, S. R. (2004). *The 7 habits of highly effective people: Powerful lessons in personal change.* Free Press.

Cuddy, A. J. C. (2018). *Presence: Bringing your boldest self to your biggest challenges.* Little, Brown and Company.

Decety, J., & Jackson, P. L. (2004). The functional architecture of human empathy. *Behavioral and Cognitive Neuroscience Reviews, 3*(2), 71–100. https://doi.org/10.1177/1534582304267187

Gardner, L., & Stough, C. (2002). Examining the relationship between leadership and emotional intelligence in senior level managers. *Leadership & Organization Development Journal, 23*(2), 68–78. https://doi.org/10.1108/01437730210419198

Gigerenzer, G., & Gaissmaier, W. (2011). Heuristic decision making. *Annual Review of Psychology, 62*, 451–482. https://doi.org/10.1146/annurev-psych-120709-145346

Gillin, P. (2019). *Attack of the customers: Why critics assault brands online and how to avoid becoming a victim.* CreateSpace Independent Publishing Platform.

Goleman, D. (1995). *Emotional intelligence: Why it can matter more than IQ.* Bantam Books.

Goleman, D., Boyatzis, R., & McKee, A. (2002). *Primal leadership: Learning to lead with emotional intelligence.* Harvard Business School Press.

Grant, A. (2013). *Give and take: Why helping others drives our success.* Viking.

Hertwig, R., & Pleskac, T. J. (2010). Recognizing rationality in the recognition heuristic. *Theory & Psychology, 20*(6), 733–766. https://doi.org/10.1177/0959354310381633

Kahneman, D. (2011). *Thinking, fast and slow.* Farrar, Straus and Giroux.

Klein, G. (1998). *Sources of power: How people make decisions.* MIT Press.

Kramer, R. M. (1999). Trust and distrust in organizations: Emerging perspectives, enduring questions. *Annual Review of Psychology, 50*(1), 569–598. https://doi.org/10.1146/annurev.psych.50.1.569

Kremer, M. R., & Hofman, E. R. (2018). Understanding the dynamics of customer relationships in business-to-business markets. *Industrial Marketing Management, 73*, 36–50. https://doi.org/10.1016/j.indmarman.2018.01.004

Maxwell, J. C. (2010). *Everyone communicates, few connect: What the most effective people do differently.* Thomas Nelson.

Morgan, R. M., & Hunt, S. D. (1994). The commitment-trust theory of relationship marketing. *Journal of Marketing, 58*(3), 20–38. https://doi.org/10.1177/002224299405800302

Salovey, P., & Mayer, J. D. (1990). Emotional intelligence. *Imagination, Cognition, and Personality, 9*(3), 185–211. https://doi.org/10.2190/DUGG-P24E-52WK-6CDG

Tannen, D. (1995). *Talking from 9 to 5: Women and men at work.* Avon.

Tickle-Degnen, L., & Rosenthal, R. (1990). The nature of rapport and its nonverbal correlates. *Psychological Inquiry, 1*(4), 285–293. https://doi.org/10.1207/s15327965pli0104_1

Voss, C. (2016). *Never split the difference: Negotiating as if your life depended on it.* Harper Business.

About the Author

Dr. Nicholas J. Pirro (DBA) is a renowned business theorist, Business Relationship Manager, and leader in operational transformation. Known for his insights on resilience, trust, and client engagement, Dr. Pirro authored *Where Are You Headed? - Get There: A Guide to Overcoming Self-Doubt for Individuals Seeking Personal and Professional Growth*, inspiring readers to break through personal barriers and achieve meaningful goals.

Dr. Pirro contributes innovative theories to the fields of business and strategy, including the Chaotic Monarch Theory and Universal Resilience Theory. His articles cover topics from the impact of AI on modern business to strategies for resilience, showcasing his commitment to advancing business thought.

A devoted husband and proud father of six, Dr. Pirro draws inspiration from his family in both his professional and personal pursuits. His commitment to community and education is evident through the Lorraine Ann Pirro Public School Endowment (LAPPSE), a fund dedicated to supporting educational initiatives in honor of his late mother. Dr. Pirro's family-centered values drive his mission to make a positive impact on the lives of others.

Connect with him on LinkedIn and explore his research on Pyrrhic Press, SSRN and ResearchGate to learn more about his work and vision.

The Art of FACT - Fast, Authentic Connections & Trus

Through genuine engagement in today's rapidly evolving world, building strong, lasting client relationships is more important than ever—and it's no longer just about sales. The Art of Fast, Authentic Connections & Trust introduces the Responsive Resonance approach, a transformative framework designed to help professionals connect quickly, engage meaningfully, and build lasting trust with clients. This book goes beyond traditional techniques, empowering you to initiate relationships with confidence, adapt to each client's unique energy, and add value at every step. Through actionable strategies and relatable insights, Dr. Nicholas J. Pirro shows how trust, empathy, and genuine engagement can turn brief encounters into sustainable partnerships. You'll learn how to: Break the ice with ease, creating a positive first impression Align with clients' communication styles to foster real connection Maintain momentum without overwhelming your clients Achieve a natural, mutually beneficial close without the hard sell Whether you're in sales, consulting, or client management, The Art of Fast, Authentic Connections & Trust provides a practical roadmap for anyone looking to deepen relationships, increase client satisfaction, and thrive in their field. Transform your approach to client engagement and build relationships that truly last.

www.ingramcontent.com/pod-product-compliance
Lightning Source LLC
LaVergne TN
LVHW040948150826
845672LV00002B/595

* 9 7 9 8 2 3 0 6 3 7 8 2 0 *